For Mackie

Text copyright © 2014 by Diane E. Muldrow
All rights reserved.
Published in the United States by Golden Books, an imprint of Random House Children's Books, a division
of Random House LLC, 1745 Broadway, New York, NY 10019, and in Canada by Random House of Canada
Limited, Toronto, Penguin Random House Companies. Golden Books, A Golden Book, A Little Golden Book,
the G colophon, and the distinctive gold spine are registered trademarks of Random House LLC. The Poky
Little Puppy is a registered trademark of Random House LLC. The artwork contained in this work was previously
published in separate works by Golden Books, New York. Copyright © 1946–1975 by Random House LLC.
Illustrations from the following Golden Books also appear herein: *Frosty the Snowman* copyright © 1950, copyright
renewed 1979 by Unichappel Music, Inc.; *The Twelve Days of Christmas: A Christmas Carol* copyright © 1992 by
Sheilah Beckett; *The Little Christmas Elf* copyright © 2011 by Susan Mitchell; and *The Golden Christmas Tree*
copyright © 1988 by Leonard Weisgard.

Holly border art on cover by Richard Scarry. Cover photo © SuperStock, Inc.

randomhouse.com/kids
dianemuldrow.com
Library of Congress Control Number: 2013957800

ISBN 978-0-553-49735-9 (trade) — ISBN 978-0-375-97374-1 (lib. bdg.) — ISBN 978-0-553-49736-6 (ebook)
PRINTED IN CHINA
10 9 8 7 6 5 4 3 2 1

Everything I Need to Know About *Christmas* I Learned From a Little Golden Book

DIANE MULDROW

A GOLDEN BOOK • NEW YORK

From *Jingle Bells* by Kathleen N. Daly,
illustrated by J. P. Miller, 1964.

CHRISTMAS is coming!

DECEMBER 1822

SUN	MON	TUE	WED	THU	FRI	SAT
1	2	3	4	5	6	7
8	9	10	11	12	13	14
15	16	17	18	19	20	21
22	23	24	**25**	26	27	28
29	30	31				

Why, it's just around the corner.

From *The Night Before Christmas* by Clement C. Moore, illustrated by Corinne Malvern, 1949.

Yikes!

From *Lucky Mrs. Ticklefeather* by Dorothy Kunhardt, illustrated by J. P. Miller, 1951.

Christmas is the most wonderful time of the year and all, but . . .

From *The Golden Book of Little Verses*,
illustrated by Mary Blair, 1953.

there's just so much to *do.*

From *The Happy Family* by Nicole, illustrated by Corinne Malvern, 1955 edition.

All that baking,

From *The Gingerbread Man* by Nancy Nolte, illustrated by Richard Scarry, 1953.

the endless cycle of cooking and cleaning,

From *Animal Friends* by Jane Werner, illustrated by Garth Williams, 1953.

and the rounds of social obligations . . .

From *My Little Golden Book About God*
by Jane Werner Watson,
illustrated by Eloise Wilkin, 1956.

when you *could* be taking a nap.

Can we just call the Christmas season
what it really is?

From *I Am a Bunny*, A Golden Sturdy Book, by Ole Risom, illustrated by Richard Scarry, 1963.

Cold and flu season!

From *Chipmunk's ABC* by Roberta Miller, illustrated by Richard Scarry, 1963.

Then there's the snarled holiday traffic . . .

From *The Taxi That Hurried* by Lucy Sprague Mitchell,
Irma Simonton Black, and Jessie Stanton, illustrated by Tibor Gergely, 1946.

and the scary holiday crowds!

From *My Little Golden Christmas Book*, illustrated by Sheilah Beckett, 1957.

From *Baby Looks* by Esther Wilkin,
illustrated by Eloise Wilkin, 1960.

Marauding relatives!

The kids are *nuts* this time of year.

From *Naughty Bunny* by Richard Scarry, 1959.

And let's not even *think* about the hassles of holiday travel.

Both pages: From *The Taxi That Hurried* by Lucy Sprague Mitchell, Irma Simonton Black, and Jessie Stanton, illustrated by Tibor Gergely, 1946.

The excess!

From *Rupert the Rhinoceros* by Carl Memling, illustrated by Tibor Gergely, 1960.

The expense!

From *5 Pennies to Spend* by Miriam Young, illustrated by Corinne Malvern, 1955.

Then comes the weight gain.

From *Noises and Mr. Flibberty-Jib* by Gertrude Crampton, illustrated by Eloise Wilkin, 1947.

It's enough to make you want to hibernate till New Year's!

From *The Golden Sleepy Book* by Margaret Wise Brown, illustrated by Garth Williams, 1948.

But then again,
think about what
you'd miss—

From *The Animals' Merry Christmas* by Kathryn Jackson, illustrated by Richard Scarry, 1958.

especially if you've been good this year.

From *Rudolph the Red-Nosed Reindeer*, adapted by Barbara Shook Hazen,
illustrated by Richard Scarry, 1958.

You'd miss all this!

From *Baby's Christmas*
by Esther Wilkin,
illustrated by Eloise Wilkin, 1959.

Christmas comes but once a year, so up and at 'em!

From "The Naughty Little Reindeer" in *The Animals' Merry Christmas*,
A Giant Golden Book, by Kathryn Jackson, illustrated by Richard Scarry, 1950.

Time to strategize!
Set up your secret wrapping station.

From *The Little Golden Holiday Book* by Marion Conger, illustrated by Eloise Wilkin, 1951.

Make your Christmas list.

DEAR SANTA —
PLEASE BRING US WARM
SWEATERS, RUBBER BALLS,
AND LOTS MORE TOYS.
— THE FIVE LITTLE
PUPPIES

From *The Poky Little Puppy's First Christmas*, A Big Golden Book,
by Adelaide Holl, illustrated by Florence Sarah Winship, 1973.

From *The Little Christmas Elf*
by Nikki Shannon Smith,
illustrated by Susan Mitchell, 2011.

Elves are standing by!

Start planning the menu.

From "The Goose That Stuffed Herself" in *The Animals' Merry Christmas*,
A Giant Golden Book, by Kathryn Jackson, illustrated by Richard Scarry, 1950.

Find the best ingredients you can,

From "The County Fair" in *Farm Stories*, A Giant Golden Book,
by Kathryn and Byron Jackson, illustrated by Gustaf Tenggren, 1946.

and make Christmas dinner
one to remember.

From *Christmas in the Country* by Barbara Collyer and John R. Foley,
illustrated by Retta Worcester, 1950.

**But don't spend *all* your
time preparing. . . .**

When was the last time you went caroling?

From *The Animals' Merry Christmas* by Kathryn Jackson, illustrated by Richard Scarry, 1958.

**Or over the river
and through the woods?**

From *Jingle Bells* by Kathleen N. Daly, illustrated by J. P. Miller, 1964.

Enjoy the season,

From *I Am a Bunny*, A Golden Sturdy Book, by Ole Risom, illustrated by Richard Scarry, 1963.

and make time for family and friends.

From *My Little Golden Christmas Book,* illustrated by Sheilah Beckett, 1957.

Why not put the kids' energy to good use?
There are decorations to make . . .

From *Trim the Christmas Tree*, A Little Golden Activity Book, by Elsa Ruth Nast,
illustrated by Doris and Marion Henderson, 1957.

and boughs to bring home!

From *The Little Golden Holiday Book* by Marion Conger, illustrated by Eloise Wilkin, 1951.

The best part of Christmas
is anticipating it together!

From *The Night Before Christmas* by Clement C. Moore, illustrated by Corinne Malvern, 1949.

Just don't overdo it.

From *Christmas in the Country* by Barbara Collyer and John R. Foley,
illustrated by Retta Worcester, 1950.

And don't forget to break for hot cocoa!

From *The Sweet Smell of Christmas*, A Golden Scratch & Sniff Book, by Patricia Scarry, illustrated by J. P. Miller, 1970.

Oh, the laughter and shouting!

From *Frosty the Snow Man* retold by Annie North Bedford, illustrated by Corinne Malvern, 1951.

From "Mr. Hedgehog's Christmas Present" in *The Animals' Merry Christmas*
by Kathryn Jackson, illustrated by Richard Scarry, 1958.

The out-and-abouting!

The writing, the mailing!

From *The Christmas ABC* by Florence Johnson, illustrated by Eloise Wilkin, 1962, renewed 1990.

The jolly wassailing!

From *The Twelve Days of Christmas: A Christmas Carol*, illustrated by Sheilah Beckett, 1992.

Christmas is about going all out . . .

From *Jingle Bells* by Kathleen N. Daly,
illustrated by J. P. Miller, 1964.

and Christmas is about keeping it simple.

From "The Singing Christmas Tree" in *The Animals' Merry Christmas* by Kathryn Jackson,
illustrated by Richard Scarry, 1958.
Facing page: From *Baby's Christmas* by Esther Wilkin, illustrated by Eloise Wilkin, 1959.

It's a time for children,

a time of wonder,

From *Christmas Carols,* illustrated by Corinne Malvern, 1946.

a time like no other time of year,

From *The Night Before Christmas* by Clement C. Moore, illustrated by Eloise Wilkin, 1955.

announced with the call of the trumpet . . .

From *Christmas Carols*,
illustrated by Corinne Malvern, 1952 edition.

**and the pealing
of bells.**

From *Christmas Carols*, illustrated by Corinne Malvern, 1946.

A time for traditions,

From *Christmas in the Country* by Barbara Collyer and John R. Foley,
illustrated by Retta Worcester, 1950.

**and cinnamon and peppermint and cloves
and orange and chocolate and ginger . . .**

From *The Sweet Smell of Christmas*, A Golden Scratch & Sniff Book,
by Patricia Scarry, illustrated by J. P. Miller, 1970.

and merriment.

From *My Little Golden Christmas Book*, cover illustration by Richard Scarry, 1957.

A time for giving the very best of yourself . . .

From "Mr. Hedgehog's Christmas Present" in *The Animals' Merry Christmas*
by Kathryn Jackson, illustrated by Richard Scarry, 1958.

a time to reach out to someone
who'd otherwise be alone . . .

From "The Goose That Stuffed Herself" in *The Animals' Merry Christmas*,
A Giant Golden Book, by Kathryn Jackson, illustrated by Richard Scarry, 1950.

and a time for blessings on all of us, every one.

From *The Kitten's Surprise* by Nina, illustrated by Feodor Rojankovsky, 1951.

So deck the halls!

From *Christmas Carols*, illustrated by Corinne Malvern, 1946.

Deck yourselves!

From *The Twelve Dancing Princesses* retold by Jane Werner, illustrated by Sheilah Beckett, 1954.

**But take some time
to be still . . .**

From *My Little Golden Book About God* by Jane Werner Watson,
illustrated by Eloise Wilkin, 1956.

on a night
quieted by snow,
and remember
another night . . .

From *The Golden Christmas Book,* by Gertrude Crampton, illustrated by Corinne Malvern, 1947.

From *The Night Before Christmas* by Clement C. Moore, illustrated by Eloise Wilkin, 1955.

From *The New Golden Song Book*, illustrated by Mary Blair, 1955 edition.

One night in a manger, under a star,

From *The Christmas Story* by Jane Werner, illustrated by Eloise Wilkin, 1952.

a night witnessed by both shepherds and kings,

when gifts were given to a waiting world. . . .

From *The Christmas Story* by Jane Werner, illustrated by Eloise Wilkin, 1952.

The gift
of love

From *The New Baby* by Ruth and Harold Shane
illustrated by Eloise Wilkin

for all people,

From *The Golden Books Treasury of Prayers from Around the World,*
selected by Esther Wilkin, illustrated by Eloise Wilkin, 1975.

**and the gift of hope
for a peaceable kingdom.**

It could happen.

From *The Golden Christmas Tree* by Jan Wahl, illustrated by Leonard Weisgard, 1988.

Believe.

From *The Night Before Christmas* by Clement C. Moore, illustrated by Corinne Malvern, 1949.